Cornerstones of Life

Practical Wisdom to Build Your Best Self

by
Michael Scott Rothman

Cornerstones of Life
Practical Wisdom to Build Your Best Self

By Michael Scott Rothman

Cover image of Bobbie Carlyle's "Self Made Man" used with the sculptor's expressed written permission.

ISBN: 978-1-7344562-0-2 Paperback

For Darlene, always

> MAN CANNOT
> REMAKE HIMSELF
> WITHOUT SUFFERING,
> FOR HE IS BOTH THE
> MARBLE AND THE
> SCULPTOR.
>
> *ALEXIS CARREL*

Introduction

All critical knowledge since time immemorial has been passed along from one person to another. It doesn't matter if we're talking about medicine, science, culinary arts, filmmaking, irrigation or fly fishing. Reflect for a minute about the times in your life when a piece of information (or a perspective) was passed along to you, and then think about how critically important it was. It could have come from your mom or dad, a coach, a teacher, an HVAC technician, or a dance instructor. I've been on the receiving end of that, and I've been on the giving end. But we're afforded only so many conversations and opportunities before the big dirt nap, so I wrote this book to pass along bits of wisdom I've found to be critical. I hope these nuggets allow you to help those you care about build a better life, which all starts by working at building a better version of yourself.

MICHAEL SCOTT ROTHMAN

> ### It's never hard to make a decision when you know what your values are.
>
> *Roy Disney*

The Inviolable Rule

Treat everyone the way you want to be treated. If we all did this, the world would be transformed. Learning how to get along with people is one of the most important skills we can develop. Given the vastness of our interactions, it seems evident that one inviolable rule is to act in accordance with the oldest of mandates—treat the other person the way *you* want to be treated. Even in very tricky situations, this works nearly-100% of the time. I once asked the head of a global research division at a large New York institution how he managed nearly 800 analysts when my wife and I struggled to manage the five children we were raising. He said it was simple—he made it a habit to always try to *do the right thing*, regardless of the situation. In that split second before you might let anger or some other feeling come to the surface, try to remember this golden rule—and make a habit of it. The world will be better off for it, and so will you.

Michael Scott Rothman

> # A CANDLE LOSES NOTHING BY LIGHTING ANOTHER CANDLE.
>
> *JAMES KELLER*

> # DON'T JUDGE EACH DAY BY THE HARVEST YOU REAP, BUT BY THE SEEDS YOU SOW.
>
> *ROBERT LOUIS STEVENSON*

Mouth to Ear

The greatest lessons and keystones of knowledge require information to be passed directly from one person to the next. It was not until late in life that I came to distill this as a timeless truth. A phrase used to describe the process is *"mouth to ear,"* a mechanism that links us to each other and to our collective past. It's not a philosophical argument about all of us being one big family—although, to be frank, we all do come from the same stardust. What I'm talking about here is being mindful of a critical tradition to share knowledge and wisdom with our family, friends, and co-workers. Most of us engage in this practice without being aware of it. But, being mindful of this tradition helps us stay grounded and keeps us connected. Whether we realize it or not, we all rely on subject matter experts. Did you ever consider that all those with specialized skills you've ever dealt with relied on those before them to build their knowledge?

MICHAEL SCOTT ROTHMAN

> # The harder I work,
> # the luckier I get.
>
> *Samuel Goldwyn*

> # Tricks and treachery are
> # the practice of fools
> # that don't have brains
> # enough to be honest.
>
> *Benjamin Franklin*

A Growth Mindset – It's Your Choice

Whatever your view is on spirituality, a great gift bestowed on us is the ability to change how we think. What we think affects how we feel. How we feel affects how we act, and how we act shapes our lives and destinies. I'm compelled to suggest that we all need to develop a *growth mindset*. The guts of this boil down to a view that we *all* have the capacity to learn just about anything we're willing to work at. We are all inherently capable of expanding various skills, and it's not just a case of the "lucky few" born with a talent to achieve greatness. Relying on a view that talent is why people succeed covers up a painful realization about our inherent laziness and a choice not to work hard enough or long enough to achieve what we desire. High achievers are those willing to work smartest and hardest at improving themselves. The only place where "success" comes before "work" is in a dictionary.

MICHAEL SCOTT ROTHMAN

> ## PEOPLE WITH GOOD INTENTIONS MAKE PROMISES, BUT PEOPLE WITH GOOD CHARACTER KEEP THEM.
>
> *RONALD OLIVER*

> ## CHALLENGES ARE WHAT MAKE LIFE INTERESTING; OVERCOMING THEM IS WHAT MAKES LIFE MEANINGFUL
>
> *JOSHUA J. MARIE*

Under-Promise, Over-Deliver

Doing the right thing doesn't mean doing what's easiest. You've got to live with the consequences of your decisions. You're reading this because you inherently want to make yourself a better person and the world a better place. One of the highest compliments to give someone is calling them a *stand-up guy*. An even higher compliment, in my opinion, is saying someone is *"as good as their word."* Make honor, courage and integrity your hallmarks. Doing the right thing is a behavior you groove into a habit. Just about all our dealings with each other are inherently based on trust. One's honor and integrity equate to a house built on a solid foundation. To distill this down even further, when you tell someone you're going to do something (whatever it is), have the courage to make damn sure you do it. Remember, the golden rule is at play here.

> # THERE IS NO EXERCISE BETTER FOR THE HEART THAN REACHING DOWN AND LIFTING PEOPLE UP.
>
> *JOHN HOLMES*

Charity is More Than Writing Checks

As a dad or a mom, a grandma or a grandpa, you may be thinking about the breadth of lessons you've been (and still are) teaching your children, grandchildren, or maybe even great-grandchildren. But how many times have you helped someone solve a problem or provided someone with a useful perspective about a troubling issue?

When we share our experiences and perspectives, we satisfy an innate need to be of service to others. There is a school of thought that in order to be happy, a person has to make *another* person happy. It's part of our biological wiring. Often, when we think about charity, financially supporting a foundation or group comes to mind. But, many of the greatest acts of charity relate to time spent counseling a family member or friend. Be unselfish with your energy.

> **IN THE BATTLE BETWEEN THE RIVER AND THE ROCK, THE RIVER ALWAYS WINS, NOT BY STRENGTH BUT BY SHEER PERSISTENCE.**
>
> *PERSIAN PROVERB*

> **SMOOTH SEAS DO NOT MAKE SKILLFUL SAILORS.**
>
> *AFRICAN PROVERB*

Find Your Passion(s)

Everyone who is successful in their profession has one thing in common: a passion for their work. Practical experience shows that the limits we place on ourselves from a fear of failure produce regret—the woulda-coulda-shoulda remarks we've said or heard someone say. In reality, there is no reward without risk. It's important to find out what you like and what you don't like. Odds are high that if you find an area of keen interest, you'll want to develop the various skills needed to succeed at it. Learning how to speak a foreign language, play a musical instrument, fly fish, and so on and so forth require an effort to get over your inherent inertia to stay at rest. If you try something and don't like it, there's really no harm in that— although skydiving without a parachute may be the exception to that rule. Make the effort to find what suits you. It's more important to want what you have than to get what you want.

Michael Scott Rothman

> ## No problem can withstand the assault of sustained thinking.
>
> *Voltaire*

> ## Never be afraid to try something new. remember, amateurs build the ark and professionals built the Titanic.
>
> *UNKNOWN*

Break Big Problems
into Little Ones

We all have the freeze-flight-fight instinct. And when we're confronted with a big issue, the limbic portion of the brain grabs the proverbial steering wheel which, in turn, suppresses the creative capacities of the cerebral cortex—the part of the brain we actually need to solve that issue. We deal with this mechanism every day, mostly because the "thinking" part of our brain is doing battle to counter impulses that arise from the "feeling" part.

When it comes to solving a major problem, there is a way to short-circuit that reptilian reflex and basically help subdue the normal limbic reaction. The most effective means to do this is to literally say out loud to yourself, *I'll figure it out.* And figure it out you will.

> **INSTINCT IS THE NOSE OF THE MIND.**
>
> *DELPHINE DE GIRARDIN*

> **YOU ONLY LIVE ONCE, BUT IF YOU DO IT RIGHT THEN ONCE IS ENOUGH.**
>
> *MAE WEST*

Trust Your Gut

Some call instinct trusting your intuition, but in reality it is simply that part of our brain that's always computing in the background and subconsciously figuring out problems before we consciously realize the answer. Many books have been written on the subject, but what I want to pass along is that when you think something is right, it usually is (and vice versa).

Sometimes we're not aware of the "why" something feels right (or wrong), and a clear answer may take time to avail itself. There's no rhyme or reason when that answer becomes evident to us—this is why keeping a pen and pad next to your bed isn't a bad tactic for when you get those "aha moments." But, until a clear reason emerges why a feeling is occurring, it's best to just trust your gut. Experience has shown that ignoring such feelings can be dangerous.

MICHAEL SCOTT ROTHMAN

> **GIVE ME SIX HOURS TO CHOP DOWN A TREE AND I WILL SPEND THE FIRST FOUR SHARPENING THE AXE.**
>
> *ABRAHAM LINCOLN*

You Really Are What You Eat

Everything that goes into your body is an impetus for change. There has been a growing recognition about the benefits of plant-based diets, but the one commonality you'll discover about all the ways to eat better is to avoid processed sugar.

A groundswell of research has concluded that processed sugar has all the characteristics of a drug. There is no benefit to consuming it, yet it is incorporated into a great deal of prepared foods.

It does take work to develop a healthy way to eat, and "kicking the sugar habit" takes genuine effort. But, if you need one thought to help change your mindset about the consumption of processed sugar, remember this: cancer is basically a weak cell that we strengthen by feeding it sugar. Your health affects everything you do, and everyone you know.

MICHAEL SCOTT ROTHMAN

> ## GOOD ACTIONS GIVE STRENGTH TO OURSELVES AND INSPIRE GOOD ACTIONS IN OTHERS.
>
> *PLATO*

> ## WHEN FACED WITH A CHALLENGE, LOOK FOR A WAY, NOT A WAY OUT.
>
> *DAVID WEATHERFORD*

Being the Leader Means
Being a Good Example

Being entrusted with a leadership role isn't about getting a special parking space, an extra piece of chicken on the chow line, or whatever. It's about the willingness to assume the responsibility for a team or group, and the proverbial cost of admission is setting a good example. Yes, the satisfaction of actually achieving a goal is a payoff, but when you're in the role of being *the boss*, it is imperative that you rely on leadership skills rather than authority.

Poor leadership is why companies go out of business, and it's the reason institutions fail. Thinking critically and communicating effectively are related skills that can be developed and honed. But setting a good example is a conscious decision that is at the forefront of a successful leader's thoughts.

MICHAEL SCOTT ROTHMAN

Cornerstone Publishing, Inc.
31 Old Farm Road
Berkeley Heights, New Jersey 07922
USA

ISBN: 978-1-7344562-0-2 Paperback

"Self Made Man" available at BobbieCarlyleSculpture.com
Contact: BobbieCarlyle@gmail.com